SLOW COOKER DUMP BBQ

SLOW
COOKER
DUMP
BBQ

EVERYDAY RECIPES FOR BARBECUE
WITHOUT THE FUSS

JENNIFER PALMER

THE COUNTRYMAN PRESS

A DIVISION OF W. W. NORTON & COMPANY

INDEPENDENT PUBLISHERS SINCE 1923

Copyright © 2017 by Jennifer Palmer

All rights reserved
Printed in the United States of America

For information about permission to reproduce selections from this book, write to Permissions, The Countryman Press, 500 Fifth Avenue, New York, NY 10110

For information about special discounts for bulk purchases, please contact W. W. Norton Special Sales at specialsales@wwnorton.com or 800-233-4830.

The Countryman Press
www.countrymanpress.com

A division of W. W. Norton & Company, Inc.,
500 Fifth Avenue, New York, NY 10110
www.wwnorton.com

978-1-58157-451-7 (pbk.)

10 9 8 7 6 5 4 3 2 1

"BARBECUE MAY NOT BE THE ROAD TO WORLD PEACE,
BUT IT'S A START."

—ANTHONY BOURDAIN

SLOW COOKER DUMP BBQ
CONTENTS

Chapter Three: Beef / 73

Chapter Four: Venison & Other Meats / 89

Chapter Five: Classic BBQ Sides / 101

Introduction

Americans love their barbecue—and slow cookers offer busy home cooks the perfect way to prepare delicious BBQ without the time-consuming hassle of using an expensive outdoor grill. *Slow Cooker Dump BBQ* is a handy (mostly) 5-ingredients-or-less slow cooker handbook that covers the essential styles of American barbecue—Carolina, Texas, Memphis, and Kansas City—with easy, no-fuss recipes the whole family will enjoy. Here you'll find more than 50 flavorful and fun recipes for pulled BBQ pork, braised beef, pulled BBQ chicken, and essential sides like cornbread, grits, and baked beans. Whether it's Fourth of July, Memorial Day, Labor Day, or just a regular weekday, cooks and families everywhere will love this easy-to-use guide for delicious barbecue recipes.

A Brief History of Barbecue

The practice of barbecue is thought to have originated in the Caribbean. Some etymologists believe the word barbecue is derived from *barabicu*, from a language spoken by the Taíno people of the Caribbean as well as the native Timucua people of Florida. The Spanish then appear to have adapted it to *barbacoa*. The first English usage of the word didn't come until 1661. Barbecue back then was pretty similar to how we know it today. A cut of meat was set on sticks and roasted above a fire. The smoke would impart the meat with flavor. The practice of barbecue was soon established in the Southern United States with pork as the primary meat, owing to the abundance of pigs in the region. Barbecue continues to be popular, owing to its affordability (no expensive cuts of meat required) and how easy it is to make—not to mention its delicious taste.

Barbecue Styles and Sauces

"Southern barbecue is the closest thing we have in the U.S. to Europe's wines or cheeses; drive a hundred miles and the barbecue changes."

—John Shelton Reed

Barbecue is a serious business. Lots of people have recipes for homemade marinades and sauces that have been handed down over the generations and which incorporate different styles and traditions. Below are some of the basic barbecue styles in the U.S. Of course there are many more regional styles and there's no one "true" way to make a barbecue sauce—despite what regional experts may tell you. At the end of the day, whatever tastes good to you and your family is what matters!

Kansas City Style

This is probably what most people think of when they hear the word "barbecue"—the thick, ketchup- or tomato-based sauce that you commonly find on ribs and sliders in restaurants and backyard grills throughout the country. It is pretty sweet and can include everything from brown sugar to molasses and honey.

Yield: About 4 cups

2 cups ketchup

2 cups water

2 tablespoons tomato paste

½ cup cider vinegar

¼ cup dark molasses

¼ cup brown sugar

1 tablespoon Worcestershire sauce

1 tablespoon chili powder

1 tablespoon salt

1 teaspoon black pepper

1 teaspoon crushed red pepper

Combine all ingredients and simmer them in a saucepan for 20 to 30 minutes.

Tip: Use this recipe in place of store-bought sauce in any of the recipes. Two cups will substitute for an 18-ounce bottle.

Texas-Style Barbecue

Texas style is light on the tomato and sugar and heavy on the spices—these thinner sauces are commonly packed with black pepper, chili pepper, cumin, fresh onion, and green pepper. Meat drippings are often added to the sauce for extra flavor.

Yield: About 1½ cups

1 tablespoon butter

½ white onion, chopped

1 cup ketchup

⅓ cup brown sugar

⅓ cup Worcestershire sauce

¼ cup lemon juice

1 chipotle chili, minced, with seeds

1 teaspoon cayenne pepper

1 teaspoon black pepper

1 teaspoon garlic powder

Melt the butter in a saucepan. Add the onion and cook until it becomes translucent. Add the remaining ingredients and simmer them for 20 to 30 minutes.

Tip: These sauces can be used as a side to any of the dishes in this book.

Low Country Carolina Style

Mustard sauce (a.k.a. Carolina Gold) is made primarily of (you guessed it) yellow mustard, plus vinegar, sugar, and spices. This mustard-style barbecue is found in southeast South Carolina and was made popular by German settlers in the area.

Yield: About 1 cup

1 cup apple cider vinegar

3 tablespoons brown sugar

2 tablespoons yellow mustard

1 teaspoon red pepper flakes

1 teaspoon ground black pepper

Combine all ingredients and simmer them in a saucepan for 20 to 30 minutes.

Carolina Variation

This vinegar-based sauce, heavy on the black pepper, is popular on the coast of North Carolina.

Yield: About 2 cups

1½ cups apple cider vinegar

3½ tablespoons hot sauce

2 tablespoons brown sugar

2 teaspoons crushed red pepper flakes

1 teaspoon black pepper

1 teaspoon cayenne pepper

Dash of liquid smoke

Combine all ingredients and simmer them in a saucepan for 20 to 30 minutes.

Stocking Your Kitchen

Shopping for BBQ recipes is very easy. Meat, sauce, and spices is usually all it takes. There are many more complicated recipes out there, of course—ones that use a lot of different spices, or ones that require a fancy backyard meat smoker with wood chips from Malta that have been dried and cured for nine years. But most of *these* recipes call for a few straightforward ingredients that are easy to find at any store. I like to have a few of these items on hand to ensure I can always throw together a delicious barbecue meal if I'm in the mood. I use a 6-quart slow cooker for all of these recipes.

1. A good Kansas-style barbecue sauce. Brands like Sweet Baby Ray's, Jack Daniel's Barbecue Sauce, or Hunt's are all common brands you can find at the grocery store. The Texas-made Stubb's Spicy Bar-B-Q is also a good option if you like your sauce spicy.

2. Ketchup.

3. Apple cider vinegar. This is a common addition to lots of barbecue dishes, especially East Carolina–style recipes.

4. Essential BBQ spices like cracked black pepper, chili powder, red pepper flakes, and cumin.

5. Your favorite mustard. I like regular yellow mustard or honey mustard. This ingredient is commonly included in Low Country Carolina–style recipes.

6. Soft white rolls. Perfect for loading up with pulled pork!

Slow Cooker BBQ tips

Use a liner: Barbecue is a messy business (and doesn't messy food somehow just taste better?), which can mean a lot of cleanup. To keep cleanup to a minimum, I recommend using a slow cooker liner for all barbecue recipes.

Drain the excess liquid (and serve on the side): If you take a peek at your meal in progress and it seems like there's too much liquid in the slow cooker, don't panic. That liquid is often soaked up during the cooking process. But feel free to drain it off. There can be many reasons for excess liquid: some barbecue sauces are thinner than others and slow cookers cook at different temperatures depending on the brand. You can also reserve the extra liquid and serve it as a dip on the side, or drizzled over the top of the meat. If it's too thin, a quick 10 to 15 minutes in a saucepan helps reduce the extra liquid. No sense in wasting it!

Add a dash of liquid smoke: Lots of barbecue lovers crave an authentic just-off-the-grill flavor. By adding a dash of liquid smoke to the mix you can give your recipe a hint of that charred, smoky flavor.

Embrace experimentation: One of my good friends swears by chicken thighs for all her slow cooker chicken recipes. She finds chicken breasts just don't work for her and can come out a bit dry. Just one of the mysteries of slow cooking, I guess! The point is, slow cooking offers lots of opportunities for innovation depending on your taste preferences, your type of slow cooker, and what you have on hand. So feel free to adapt and add your own twist to these recipes. And remember to have fun!

CHAPTER ONE

PORK

BBQ-Cola Ribs

Every Southerner knows the secret ingredient to good BBQ is a can of cola. In this case, a half can of Coca-Cola Classic will give our ribs a sweet, flavorful taste that can't be beat. As the slogan says: "Things go better with Coke!"

Yield: 4–6 servings   Cook time: 4 hours

3 pounds pork back ribs

⅛ teaspoon salt

⅛ teaspoon pepper

One 18-ounce bottle barbecue sauce, or 2 cups homemade

½ can Coca-Cola (6 ounces of a 12-ounce can)

Cut the rack of ribs in half. Sprinkle the ribs with salt and pepper and add them to a lined slow cooker, positioning them so that they lean against the sides. Combine the BBQ sauce and Coke in bowl, then pour the mixture over ribs. Cover and cook on high for 4 hours or on low for 8 hours.

Straight-Up Dry Rub Pork Roast with Onions

Sometimes you're not in the mood for overly sloppy or saucy BBQ. That's where dry rubs come in. This recipe results in tender, juicy pork with intense, full flavors thanks to the onions and the spices in the dry rub—and you won't need a bib and wet wipes to enjoy it! Serve with a heap of mashed potatoes or pile on a roll for a juicy roast pork sandwich.

Yield: 4–6 servings   Cook Time: 8 hours

1 onion, peeled and sliced into rings

One 3- to 4-pound pork butt roast

3 tablespoons store-bought dry rub

2 tablespoons brown sugar

Squeeze of lime

Add the onion rings to the bottom of a lined slow cooker. Place the pork on top. Combine the dry rub and brown sugar. Using your fingers, rub the meat thoroughly with the sugar/rub mixture. Cover and cook on low for 8 hours or until the meat is soft and pulls apart easily with a fork. Add a squeeze of lime to each serving for a bit of citrus tang.

"My first outdoor cooking memories are full of erratic British summers, Dad swearing at a barbecue that he couldn't put together, and eventually eating charred sausages, feeling brilliant."

—Jamie Oliver

East Carolina Pulled Pork

This is a classic, vinegar-based Eastern Carolina pork barbecue recipe. Well, as classic as you can get when it's made in a slow cooker! If you like your barbecue with a bit more heat, trying adding a teaspoon or two of cayenne pepper. Or add a dash of liquid smoke to give it that fresh-from-the-smokehouse flavor.

Yield: 6–8 servings   Cook Time: 13 hours

One 5-pound bone-in pork shoulder roast

1 tablespoon mixed salt and pepper

1½ cups apple cider vinegar

3½ tablespoons hot sauce

2 tablespoons brown sugar

2 teaspoons crushed red pepper flakes

Cayenne pepper (optional)

Liquid smoke (optional)

6–8 rolls, sliced

Prepared coleslaw (optional)

Place the roast, salt and pepper mixture, and vinegar in a lined slow cooker and cook on low for 12 hours. Remove the pork from the cooker and discard the bones. Drain the excess liquid, reserving 2 cups. Shred the pork and return it to the slow cooker. Mix the hot sauce, brown sugar, pepper flakes, and reserved liquid. If you decide to add the optional cayenne pepper and/ or liquid smoke, do so now. Pour the mixture over the shredded pork and stir. Cook on low for one hour and serve on rolls, garnished with coleslaw, if desired.

Apricot BBQ Po'boys

Sweet apricots, together with pulled pork and a hint of fresh onion, ensure these Louisiana-style po'boys will be a hit with the whole family. Heap onto a crisp white roll and serve with the remaining sauce for dipping.

Yield: 4–6 servings   Cook Time: 8 hours

One 3-pound pork shoulder, boneless

1 cup sweet onion, chopped

One 18-ounce bottle barbecue sauce, or 2 cups homemade

1 cup apricot jam

2 tablespoons cider vinegar

2 tablespoons brown sugar

1 tablespoon Worcestershire sauce

4–6 rolls, sliced

Add the pork shoulder and onion to a lined slow cooker. Mix the remaining ingredients in a bowl and pour them over the pork. Cook on low for 8–10 hours.

Pulled Pork
Avocado Bowl

This is a fresh and flavorful alternative to traditional barbecue. The red cabbage adds a light crunch while the avocado packs a healthy punch of essential fatty acids. Heap the pulled pork into a bowl until it's nearly full, add a layer of salsa, and top with avocado slices. This recipe is great for a quick lunch or dinner—and it's an easy way to use those pulled pork leftovers in the fridge.

Yield: 4–6 servings   Cook Time: 8 hours

One 2-pound pork shoulder roast

½ cup ketchup

½ cup brown sugar

⅓ cup apple cider vinegar

1 cup fresh salsa

2 avocados, sliced

Add the roast, ketchup, brown sugar, and vinegar to a lined slow cooker. Cook on low for 8 hours. Shred the meat and add it to a personal-sized bowl. Heap a big scoop of fresh salsa over the meat and top with the avocado slices.

Classic BBQ
Pork Chops

This is a very simple recipe for tender, juicy pork chops that makes for a quick, easy meal. Serve with your favorite side—I love these with mashed potatoes and braised collard greens.

Yield: 6–8 servings   Cook time: 3-4 hours

One 18-ounce bottle barbecue sauce, or 2 cups homemade

1 tablespoon garlic powder

1 tablespoon onion powder

8 medium-sized pork chops

Add ½ cup of water to the bottom of a lined slow cooker to prevent sticking or burning. Mix the barbecue sauce, garlic powder, and onion powder. Add the pork chops and cover with the barbecue sauce mixture. Cook on high for 3 to 4 hours. Place chops under a broiler for a few minutes to brown, if you wish.

Chipotle Peach Ribs

Smoky chipotle and peach complement each other to create a sizzling sweet sauce for these tender pork ribs. Add a finely chopped chipotle pepper (I like the canned ones that come in adobo sauce) for extra kick if you really want to spice things up!

Yield: 4–6 servings   Cook Time: 6 hours

3 pounds pork loin ribs

½ cup barbecue sauce

½ cup peach jam

2 tablespoon brown sugar

2 tablespoons chipotle pepper hot sauce

Cut the ribs into single serve portions (2 to 3 ribs per portion) and place them under the broiler for 10 minutes, then add them to a lined slow cooker. Combine the remaining ingredients in a bowl and pour the mixture over the ribs. Cook on low for 6 hours. Serve the chipotle pepper sauce on the side or pour it over the ribs before serving.

"Whenever I travel to the South, the first thing I do is visit the best barbecue place between the airport and my hotel."
—Jeffrey Steingarten

Texas-Style
Pulled Pork

Spices, vinegar, and mustard make for a delicious Texas-style pulled pork recipe. This one has a few more ingredients than other recipes because of all the spices required to make a true "Texas-style" barbecue.

Yield: 6–8 servings   Cook Time: 6 hours

One 4-pound pork shoulder roast

1 cup barbecue sauce

1 cup apple cider vinegar

1 tablespoon yellow mustard

1 tablespoon Worcestershire sauce

1 onion, chopped

1 tablespoon chili powder

1 teaspoon cumin

6–8 rolls, sliced

2 cups cabbage, shredded

Add all the ingredients to a lined slow cooker and cook on high for 6 hours or on low for 10 hours. Serves on rolls, garnish with cabbage, if desired.

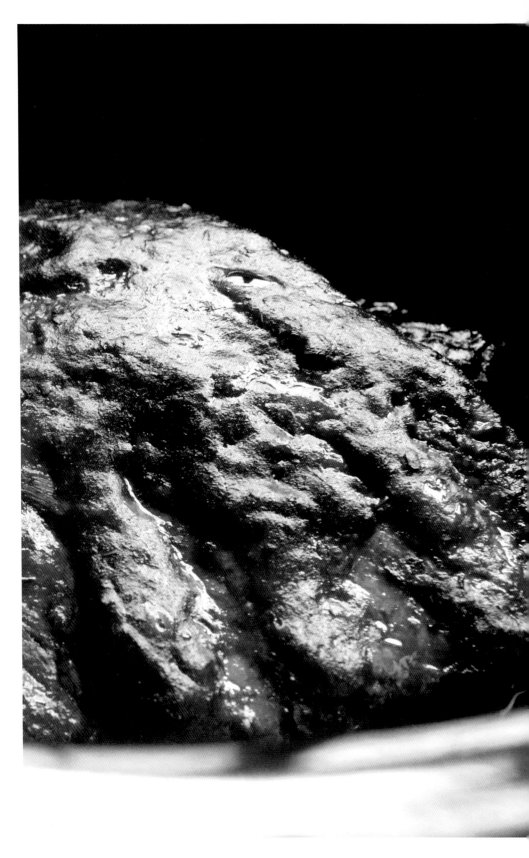

Kansas City Baby Back Ribs

Sweet, tender, and straightforward, these Kansas City-style ribs are a classic addition to any party.

Yield: 4–6 servings   Cook Time: 8 hours

3 pounds baby back ribs

One 18-ounce bottle barbecue sauce, or 2 cups homemade

½ onion, sliced

1 tablespoon garlic powder

Add ½ cup water to a lined slow cooker. Add the ribs and cover them with barbecue sauce as well as the onion and garlic powder. Cook on low for 8 hours.

Carolina-Style
Cider Roast with Vegetables

Apple cider vinegar gives this pork roast a delicious flavor, plus the carrots and onions make this a satisfying meal. No sides required—although I must say it goes very nicely with a big heap of mashed potatoes.

Yield: 4–6 servings   Cook Time: 6 hours

2 large onions, chopped

2 stalks celery, chopped

4 large carrots, chopped

1 red or yellow pepper, chopped

One 3-pound pork loin roast

1 ½ cups apple cider vinegar

2 cloves garlic, chopped

½ teaspoon black pepper

½ teaspoon ground ginger

Put onions, celery, carrot, and pepper in a lined slow cooker. Add pork roast and remaining ingredients. Cook on low for 6 hours. Drain and serve the roast and vegetables together.

Boozy Beer
Pulled Pork

This simple recipe for pulled pork gets a hint of flavor thanks to a can of beer! Barbecue goes nicely with a light beer, but whatever you have on hand will do. Some people swear by adding a heavier or more flavorful beer like a stout or ale to their barbecue sauce—so have fun experimenting!

Yield: 6–8 servings   Cook Time: 8 hours

One 4-pound pork butt roast

One 18-ounce bottle barbecue sauce, or 2 cups homemade

1 tablespoon onion powder

1 tablespoon garlic powder

1 teaspoon black pepper

One 12-ounce can light beer

6–8 rolls, sliced

Add the roast to a lined slow cooker. Mix together the barbecue sauce, onion powder, garlic powder, and pepper and pour the mixture over the roast. Add the beer to the slow cooker and cook on low for 8 to 10 hours. Shred the meat and serve.

Hawaiian Pork
Shoulder Roast

Barbecue done "Hawaiian-style" is called Kālua, and it involves placing meat wrapped in banana leaves in an underground oven called an imu. For this recipe, the slow cooker serves as an imu—no underground cooking required. Here, simple ingredients impart the pork with a smoky, salted flavor while the banana mimics the flavor traditionally provided by the banana leaves. Serve with coleslaw or slices of fresh pineapple.

Yield: 6–8 servings   Cook Time: 11 hours

One 6-pound pork shoulder roast

1 tablespoon Hawaiian sea salt

1 tablespoon liquid smoke

1 banana, unpeeled

1 teaspoon red pepper flakes

2 cups rice, prepared

Rub the roast with the salt and liquid smoke. Place the roast in a lined slow cooker. Peel the banana one-quarter of the way down the fruit and add it to the slow cooker. Cook on low for 10 hours. Remove the banana. Remove the roast from the slow cooker and shred it with a fork. Skim the fat from the remaining juice in the slow cooker. Return the pork to the defatted juice and cook for an additional hour. Top with red pepper flakes and serve over rice.

Tip: Be sure to use Hawaiian sea salt (available online or from specialty retailers), as it is softer and milder than regular sea salt.

Pulled Pork Sweet Honey Sliders

If hot and spicy barbecue isn't your thing, try this recipe, which offers a mild but flavorful alternative. Honey and brown sugar make for a sweet combination and this pork goes great on a fresh white roll with a couple of sweet pickles on top. I add a final drizzle of honey before serving.

Yield: 4–6 servings   Cook Time: 7 hours

One 3-pound pork shoulder roast, boneless

1 cup ketchup

½ cup honey

¼ cup balsamic vinegar

¼ cup brown sugar

4-6 rolls, sliced

Add the pork to a lined slow cooker. Mix the remaining ingredients together and add the mixture to the slow cooker. Cook on low for 6 hours. Shred the pork and return it to cooker for an additional hour. Serve on rolls.

Sweet Plum
BBQ Ribs

Barbecue comes in many delicious styles and this one takes its inspiration from Asian spices and flavors. Plum jelly, soy sauce, and ginger make a robust, satisfying sauce for the pork. Garnish with chopped fresh spring onion and serve over rice.

Yield: 4–6 servings   Cook Time: 6 hours

3 pounds pork loin back ribs

½ cup plum jelly

⅓ cup soy sauce

¼ cup brown sugar

2 tablespoons molasses

2 teaspoons ginger powder

Cut the ribs into 2- to 3-rib sections and broil them for 10 minutes. Add the ribs to a lined slow cooker. Combine the other ingredients in a bowl and pour the mixture over the ribs. Cook on low for 6 hours.

Tip: For a thicker sauce, try simmering the remaining slow cooker juices in a saucepan for 10 to 15 minutes.

Bourbon Apple
Pork Ribs

Tart apples, smoky bourbon, and tender pork combine to make a delicious meal that's ideal for tailgate parties, backyard gatherings, and even Thanksgiving. Perfect for fall when apples are ripe for the picking!

Yield: 4–6 servings   Cook Time: 6 hours

4 pounds pork ribs

1 cup applesauce

¾ cup bourbon

½ cup packed brown sugar

½ cup bottled barbecue sauce

½ cup apple cider vinegar

3 apples, peeled and sliced

Add the ribs to a lined slow cooker. Mix the applesauce, bourbon, brown sugar, barbecue sauce, and vinegar in a bowl and pour the mixture over the ribs. Cook the ribs on low for 3 hours, then add the apple slices and cook for an additional 3 hours.

CHAPTER TWO

CHICKEN

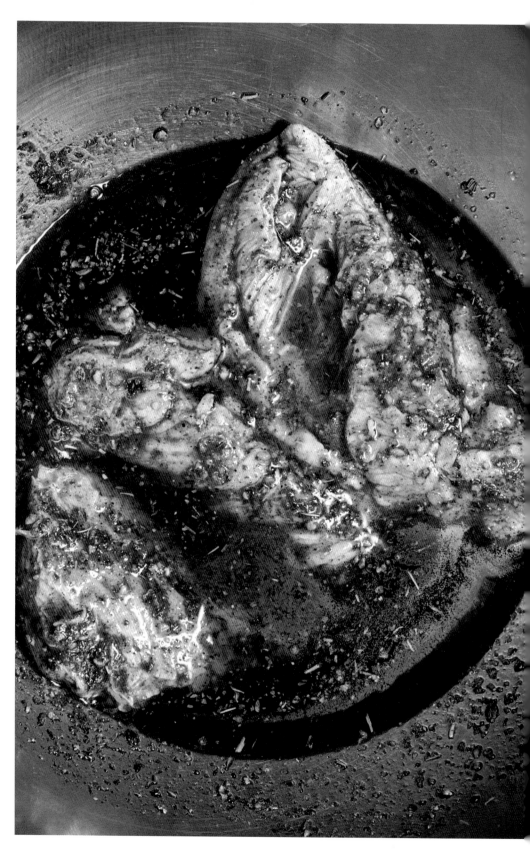

Classic BBQ Chicken

While pork might be the king of barbecue I find many classic BBQ sauces complement chicken even better than pork or other meats. When the weather is sweltering hot, this light chicken BBQ recipe is a nice alternative to pork. For extra spice, add some red pepper flakes.

Yield: 6–8 servings   Cook Time: 4 hours

4 boneless chicken breasts

One 18-ounce bottle barbecue sauce, or 2 cups homemade

¼ cup white vinegar

¼ cup brown sugar

1 tablespoon hot sauce

Red pepper flakes (optional)

Add the chicken to a lined slow cooker. Mix the remaining ingredients until the sugar is dissolved and pour the mixture over the chicken. Cook on low for 4 to 6 hours.

Smoky Pulled-Chicken Sandwiches

When we think barbecue we usually think of pork or brisket—so these pulled-chicken sandwiches are a great option if you want to change things up a bit! You can still get that smoky BBQ flavor by adding a dash of liquid smoke. Top with pickles or coleslaw for crunch! Serve with a side of creamed corn.

Yield: 6–8 servings   Cook Time: 8 hours

> 4 to 5 pounds boneless, skinless chicken breasts
>
> ¼ cup brown sugar
>
> One 18-ounce bottle barbecue sauce, or 2 cups homemade
>
> 1 teaspoon liquid smoke
>
> ½ cup water
>
> 6–8 rolls, sliced

Place the chicken in a lined slow cooker. Mix the sugar, BBQ sauce, liquid smoke, and water in a bowl. Add the mixture on top of the chicken. Cook on low for 8 hours or on high for 6 hours. Uncover and shred the chicken with two forks. Cook the shredded chicken for another 30 minutes. Pile the BBQ on top of your favorite rolls and add some toppings for crunch.

Sweet Peach
BBQ Chicken

Peaches and barbecue are a surprisingly good match. The fruit is juicy, a bit messy, and delicious. If they're in season, fresh peaches are great. Otherwise, a can of peaches will add the same delicious flavor.

Yield: 4–6 servings   Cook Time: 6 hours

3 pounds chicken drumsticks

1 ½ cups barbecue sauce, either store-bought or homemade

½ cup peach jam

2 teaspoons yellow mustard

2 peaches, peeled and sliced, or one 15-ounce can peaches

Add the chicken to a lined slow cooker. Mix the barbecue sauce, jam, and mustard in a bowl and add to the slow cooker. Cook on low for 6 to 8 hours. Add peach slices and cook for 15 additional minutes.

Tip: After cooking, the remaining sauce in the slow cooker may be a bit runny. Try thickening the sauce by simmering it in a saucepan for a few minutes. Pour it over the chicken and serve.

"Life is better than death, I believe, if only because it is less boring, and because it has fresh peaches in it."

—Alice Walker

Mango Chutney
BBQ Chicken Thighs

Fruit chutneys pack a lot of sweet flavor, so they make a nice addition to chicken. You can find mango chutney in your local grocery store with the jams and jellies or in the international grocery aisle. These BBQ chicken thighs make a light alternative for hot summer days or a comforting meal when it's cold outside. Serve over rice with a squeeze of lime.

Yield: 4–6 servings   Cook Time: 4 hours

3 pounds chicken thighs

½ cup mango chutney

1 cup barbecue sauce, store-bought or homemade

1 tablespoon onion powder

1 teaspoon curry powder

Add the chicken to a lined slow cooker. Mix the chutney, barbecue sauce, onion powder, and curry powder together, and pour it over the chicken. Cook on low for 4 to 6 hours or until the meat is fall-off-the-bone tender.

TIP: After cooking, stick the chicken under the broiler for a few minutes to crisp up the skin.

White Wine
BBQ Chicken

I guess you could say this barbecue recipe has a French influence. This takes classic chicken barbecue and elevates it with a hint of white wine. Throw all the ingredients in your slow cooker and wait for the delicious results. Serve over lettuce with a glass of white wine and pretend you're relaxing in a café somewhere in the south of France.

Yield: 4–6 servings   Cook Time: 4 hours

4 boneless chicken breasts

One 10-ounce bag frozen corn

¼ cup white wine

1 tablespoon garlic powder

One 18-ounce bottle barbecue sauce

Boston lettuce, to serve

Add the chicken and corn to a lined slow cooker. Mix the wine, garlic powder, and barbecue sauce together and pour the mixture over the chicken. Cook on low for 4 hours. Shred the chicken and serve over lettuce.

Honey Mustard Chicken with Quinoa

Quinoa is packed with good proteins and its mild, nutty flavor complements this honey mustard chicken well. Be careful not to overcook the quinoa. Serve with a fresh green salad or braised collard greens.

Yield: 4–6 servings   Cook Time: 4 hours

- 4 medium chicken breasts, fresh or defrosted
- 1 teaspoon salt
- 1 teaspoon pepper
- 1 cup quinoa, soaked and drained
- 1½ cups chicken broth
- 1 teaspoon onion powder
- 3 tablespoons honey mustard

Rub the chicken breasts with salt and pepper. Add the quinoa, chicken broth, and onion powder to a lined slow cooker and stir. Place the seasoned chicken on top of the quinoa and top with the mustard. Cook on low for 4 hours. Use a spatula to scrape the sides of the slow cooker to keep the quinoa from sticking while cooking.

Tip: If you use frozen chicken, I recommend defrosting it first so the chicken and quinoa cook at about the same pace.

BBQ Chicken Thighs with Potatoes & Olives

A hearty meal for the whole family! This chicken with roasted potatoes and green beans creates a well-rounded dish with protein, carbs, and veggies all rolled into one. The BBQ sauce and onion infuse this dish with a mild, full flavor that will satisfy any taste.

Yield: 4–6 servings   Cook Time: 7 hours

3 pounds chicken thighs

One 18-ounce bottle barbecue sauce, or 2 cups homemade

4 potatoes, chopped

1 white onion, chopped

½ cup olives

Add the chicken, sauce, potatoes, and onion to a lined slow cooker. Cook on low for 6 hours. Add the olives and cook an additional 1 to 2 hours, or until the potatoes are tender.

Zesty Chicken
Sliders

Adding Italian dressing to a classic barbecue recipe gives this chicken a bit of zip. This makes a fantastic sandwich with blue cheese crumbles and a side of crunchy slaw. Is your mouth watering yet?

Yield: 6 servings   Cook Time: 6 hours

6 boneless chicken breasts

1 cup barbecue sauce, store-bought or homemade

1 cup Italian salad dressing

¼ cup brown sugar

2 tablespoons Worcestershire sauce

1 red onion, chopped

1 teaspoon dried thyme

6 rolls, sliced

Add the chicken to a lined slow cooker. Mix the remaining ingredients and pour them over the chicken. Cook on low 6 hours. Shred the chicken and serve on a roll.

BBQ Chicken Wings

Wings are an essential snack for celebrations of any kind. Whether it's a birthday party or game day these delicious, saucy wings will be a hit. Popping them in the broiler before slow cooking them is the key. That heat makes for a crisper, more satisfying wing.

Yield: 4–6 servings   Cook Time: 4 hours

3 pounds chicken wings

One 18-ounce bottle barbecue sauce, or 2 cups homemade

¼ cup honey

1 tablespoon hot sauce

1 tablespoon Worcestershire sauce

Broil the wings for 15 minutes in the oven. Transfer the wings to a lined slow cooker and add the remaining ingredients. Cook on low for 4 to 5 hours.

Honey Mustard
BBQ Chicken

Low Country mustard-based barbecue is an easy alternative to the popular Kansas City style.

Yield: 4 servings   Cook Time: 7 hours

4 boneless chicken breasts

One 18-ounce bottle barbecue sauce, or 2 cups homemade

1 cup honey mustard

Add the ingredients to a lined slow cooker and cook for 6 hours on low. Remove and shred the chicken, and return the shredded chicken to the slow cooker.

BBQ Root Beer
Chicken

When I was growing up, drinking root beer was a special treat. My parents would take me to the A&W drive-in and order a big frosty mug, which we'd guzzle in the car along with a few burgers. The point is—root beer is delicious and it makes a great base for this sweet BBQ chicken recipe. Shred the chicken, heap it onto a roll, and enjoy!

Yield: 4 servings   Cook Time: 6 hours

4 chicken breasts

One 18-ounce bottle barbecue sauce

One 12-ounce can root beer

Squeeze of lime

Add the chicken, barbecue sauce, and root beer to a lined slow cooker. Cook on low for 4 hours or until the chicken shreds easily with a fork. Add a squeeze of lime and serve!

Apple Cider
BBQ Chicken

Apple cider vinegar makes this North Carolina–style sauce really pop! The resulting tangy barbecue chicken goes great with crunchy coleslaw and a heap of sweet and sour pickles.

Yield: 4 servings   Cook Time: 4 hours

4 boneless chicken breasts

One 18-ounce bottle barbecue sauce, or 2 cups homemade

1 cup apple cider vinegar

4 rolls, sliced

1 cup prepared coleslaw

Add all the ingredients to a lined slow cooker and cook on low for 4 hours. Shred the chicken and serve on a roll with coleslaw.

CHAPTER THREE

BEEF

Classic Chuck Roast

A classic chuck roast can be just what the doctor ordered when you've got a busy week ahead. Make this on Sunday and you'll have extra for sandwiches during the week. Plus, the delicious roast mixed with garlic and onion will make your kitchen smell amazing. Serve with a side of braised collard greens.

Yield: 4–6 servings   Cook Time: 7 hours

One 3-pound boneless chuck roast

1 tablespoon onion powder

1 tablespoon garlic powder

One 18-ounce bottle BBQ sauce, or 2 cups homemade

1 tablespoon Worcestershire sauce

Place the roast into a lined slow cooker. Rub the garlic powder and onion powder over the roast and ensure it's completely covered. Add the BBQ and Worcestershire sauces. Cook on low for 6 hours. Drain any excess juice and fat if desired. Shred the meat with a fork and cook 1 additional hour.

"Comfort is key for a barbecue."

—Ashley Madekwe, actress

Classic BBQ
Ground Beef

If you love sloppy joes like I do, this is the recipe for you. Serve atop a soft white roll and don't forget the wet wipes! I like this with a dash of barbecue sauce added. Serve with a side of mac and cheese.

Yield: 4–6 servings   Cook Time: 6 hours

2 pounds ground beef

3 cups ketchup

¼ cup brown sugar

1 tablespoon onion powder

1 tablespoon garlic powder

2 tablespoons mustard

4–6 rolls, sliced

Barbecue sauce to serve (optional)

Brown the ground beef in a frying pan for about 10-15 minutes. Drain the grease, break up the meat, and add to a lined slow cooker with the rest of the ingredients. Cook on low for 6 hours. Add a dash of barbecue sauce if desired and serve on a roll.

BBQ Beef with Bacon & Black Beans

Bacon just makes everything better, doesn't it? The flavor from the bacon strips gives the black beans and beef a full, savory flavor, and the dash of liquid smoke will make you think the meat just came off the grill. Serve over rice or noodles.

Yield: 4–6 servings   Cook Time: 8 hours

3 pounds boneless beef chuck, diced

6 slices bacon, diced

1 cup dry black beans, soaked overnight and drained

One 18-ounce bottle barbecue sauce, or 2 cups homemade

1 tablespoon apple cider vinegar

Dash of liquid smoke

Add all the ingredients to a lined slow cooker and cook on low for 8 hours. Drain and serve.

Ale & Onion
BBQ Brisket

Hearty and delicious, this brisket gets that "special something" from a generous helping of good old English (or American) ale. Serve with traditional English "chips" or a side of mac and cheese.

Yield: 4–6 servings   Cook Time: 10 hours

One 3-pound beef brisket, boneless

One 18-ounce bottle barbecue sauce, or 2 cups homemade

One 12-ounce can English or American ale

2 white onions, sliced

2 tablespoons brown sugar

1 tablespoon onion powder

Add all the ingredients to lined slow cooker and cook on low for 10 hours.

Classic Family Friendly Chili

This is a great base recipe for chili that you can modify to suit your family's tastes. It's straightforward and mild, but still has a nice, full flavor. If you like, add more chili powder or a dash of cayenne to crank up the heat! I like to serve this as a side with pulled pork sliders and jalapeño cornbread.

Yield: 4 servings   Cook Time: 8 hours

1 pound ground beef

One 14.5-ounce can stewed tomatoes

One 10.75-ounce can tomato puree

Two 15-ounce cans kidney beans, drained

2 cups diced onion

1 tablespoon chili powder

Salt and pepper to taste

Brown the beef in a skillet and drain the grease. Add the beef and the remaining ingredients into a lined slow cooker. Cook on low for 8 hours.

Tip: For a healthier option, try lean ground turkey instead of beef.

Coffee-Rub Texas Beef Brisket

Classic Texas BBQ dry rub with a twist: coffee!

Yield: 6–8 servings   Cook Time: 8 hours

One 3-pound beef brisket, boneless

2 teaspoons liquid smoke

3 tablespoons store-bought dry rub

1 tablespoon ground coffee

1 tablespoon kosher salt

1 tablespoon dark brown sugar

1 teaspoon freshly ground black pepper

Pat brisket with a paper towel until it's dry. Rub liquid smoke over the brisket. Combine the dry ingredients in a bowl and rub them evenly over the brisket, ensuring it's completely covered. Add the brisket to a lined slow cooker and cook on low for 8 hours.

BBQ Meatballs

A twist on traditional Italian meatballs, this recipe calls for beef meatballs slow cooked in tangy barbecue sauce. No tomato sauce required! They make great sliders—just add a few pickles and serve on a soft white roll.

Yield: 4-6 servings   Cook Time: 3 to 4 hours

One 28-ounce package frozen beef or pork meatballs

One 18-ounce bottle barbecue sauce, or 2 cups homemade

1 tablespoon Worcestershire sauce

¼ cup brown sugar

Add all the ingredients to a lined slow cooker. Cook on low for 3 to 4 hours.

CHAPTER FOUR

VENISON & OTHER MEATS

Shredded Venison
Sliders

Barbecue isn't just about pork and chicken. Here are some recipes for many differ-ent kinds of delicious meat—and one recipe with no meat at all! Whether you're a venison lover or still not quite sold on the taste, this recipe makes a tender, flavorful venison—without the gamey flavor—that the whole family will love. Serve on a roll and top with crunchy coleslaw.

Yield: 6–8 servings   Cook Time: 6 hours

One 3-pound venison roast

1 cup ketchup

¼ cup brown sugar

1 tablespoon mustard

1 tablespoon onion powder

Dash of liquid smoke (optional)

6–8 rolls, sliced

Prepared coleslaw (optional)

Add the roast to a lined slow cooker. Mix the remaining ingredients and pour them over the roast. Cook on low for 5 to 6 hours. Remove the roast from the slow cooker and shred the meat. Drain and reserve the liquid from the slow cooker. Return the shredded meat to the slow cooker and add the reserved liquid until desired saturation is reached. Cook 1 additional hour and serve on rolls with prepared coleslaw, if desired.

BBQ Goose Breast
Sammies

If you have a hunter in the family (or friends who are nice enough to share their bounty with you), you also probably have a freezer full of goose breast. This recipe produces a heap of tender, succulent goose meat rich with great barbecue flavor. Serve on a roll with coleslaw or heaped onto a plate with mashed potatoes.

Yield: 4 servings   Cook Time: 7 hours

2–3 goose breasts (about 2 lbs)

2 cups chicken broth

1 tablespoon onion powder

2 tablespoons butter

One 18-ounce bottle barbecue sauce, or 2 cups homemade

4 rolls, sliced

Prepared coleslaw (optional)

Add the goose breast, chicken broth, onion powder, and butter to a lined slow cooker. Cook on low for 6 hours. Shred the meat and return it to the slow cooker. Add the barbecue sauce and cook for 1 additional hour. Serve on rolls with coleslaw, if desired.

Slow Cooker
Buffalo Brisket

Bison takes a bit longer to cook than other meats, so it will require 10 hours to make a nice tender brisket. If you're a bison lover like I am, though, it's well worth the wait.

Yield: 4–6 servings   Cook Time: 10 hours

One 3-pound buffalo brisket

1 tablespoon onion powder

1 tablespoon garlic powder

3 cups chicken broth

One 18-ounce bottle barbecue sauce, or 2 cups homemade

Add the brisket, onion powder, garlic powder, and broth to a lined slow cooker. Cook on low for 10 hours. Remove the brisket and cut into thin slices. Drain the slow cooker and discard the liquid. Return the meat to the slow cooker and add the barbecue sauce. Continue cooking until the meat is ready to serve, up to 1 hour.

"Brisket is a real family and friends meal."

—Nach Waxman

Jackfruit BBQ "Pulled Pork"

Okay, so this is a recipe for meatless barbecue. That concept may make you want to run screaming the other way (or at least turn the page), but it's a great dish for vegetarians and the texture really is like pulled pork! Top with crunchy slaw to complement the soft texture of the shredded jackfruit. Make sure you buy young, green canned jackfruit for the best results. Check your local Asian supermarket or order it from an online retailer.

Yield: 4 servings   Cook Time: 6 hours

Two 20-ounce cans young, green jackfruit in water

1 cup BBQ sauce

2 tablespoons brown sugar

1 teaspoon garlic powder

½ teaspoon chili powder

4 rolls, sliced

Prepared coleslaw, for topping

Rinse and drain the jackfruit. De-core the jackfruit and chop them into pieces. Add the jackfruit and all the remaining ingredients to a lined slow cooker and stir until well mixed. Cook on low for 6 to 7 hours or until the jackfruit shreds easily with a fork. Serve the shredded "meat" on a roll and top with crunchy slaw.

BBQ Turkey Legs & Apples

Enjoying a delicious, giant turkey leg brings back childhood memories of the local county fair or the giant amusement parks you had to drive 5 hours to get to.

Yield: 3–4 servings   Cook Time: 6 hours

One 18-ounce bottle barbecue sauce

1 tablespoon apple cider vinegar

1 teaspoon garlic powder

Salt and pepper to taste

3–4 turkey legs, depending on size

1 red onion, sliced

2 large potatoes, chopped

2 apples, cored and sliced into wedges

10 prunes (optional)

Combine the barbecue sauce, 1 cup of water, apple cider vinegar, garlic powder, and salt and pepper and stir until mixed. Add the turkey legs, potatoes, and onion to a lined slow cooker and cover with sauce mixture. Cook on low for 3 hours. Add the apples and prunes, if using, and cook an additional 3 hours.

CHAPTER FIVE

CLASSIC BBQ SIDES

Creamed Corn

Barbecue lovers know that the sides are half the fun of eating barbecue. Whether it's cornbread, green beans, or this delicious recipe for creamed corn, these delicious extras will keep you and your family coming back for more (until they get full, that is—which won't take long!). Creamy, rich, and delicious—this decadent corn side goes great with any barbecue.

Yield: 4–6 servings   Cook Time: 4 hours

1 cup heavy whipping cream

One 8-ounce package cream cheese, softened

¼ cup butter

2 tablespoons granulated sugar

Salt and pepper to taste

5 cups frozen sweet corn

Parmesean cheese, grated, for serving

Add the whipping cream, cream cheese, butter, sugar, and salt and pepper to a lined slow cooker. Cook on high for 10 minutes, stirring until everything is melted. Add the sweet corn and cook on low for 4 hours. Season with Parmesan and additional salt and pepper.

BBQ Baked Beans

Beans and barbecue are an essential pairing, so try this classic baked bean recipe and serve it alongside your favorite barbecue. And feel free to get creative. This recipe just cries out for your own personal touch—add some dry mustard, garlic, or diced salt pork to take this classic recipe from traditional to out-of-this-world.

Yield: 6–8 servings   Cook Time: 8 hours

3 cups dry navy beans, soaked overnight and drained

1½ cups ketchup

1½ cups water

¼ cup molasses

1 cup chopped onion

1 cup brown sugar

Salt and pepper to taste

Add all the ingredients to a lined slow cooker and stir. Cook on low for 8 to 10 hours. Add salt and pepper to taste.

Stone Ground Grits

The first time I tried grits was in a family restaurant in Greenwood, South Carolina. And boy was I hooked. Born-and-raised Southerners probably already have a favorite way to prepare grits—but for everyone else this recipe is a great go-to. Enjoy your grits for breakfast with a side of scrambled eggs or serve with delicious BBQ anytime!

Yield: 4–6 servings   Cook Time: 6 hours

1½ cups stone ground grits

6 cups water

2 teaspoons salt

2 cups whole milk

4 tablespoons butter

One 12-ounce package grated cheddar cheese (optional)

Combine the grits, water, and salt and add to a lined slow cooker. Cook on low for 6 to 8 hours. Stir occasionally, if possible, to keep the grits from sticking to the sides of the slow cooker. Before serving, add the milk, butter, and the optional cheese (if desired). Cook for 15 minutes, or until the cheese and butter have melted.

Tip: I love using stone ground grits, but any kind of grits will do.

"I'll bring my grits when I travel, because I get so hungry on the road."
—Dolly Parton

Slow Cooker
Cornbread

Making cornbread in a slow cooker may seem a bit tricky at first, but this is a quick and easy way to enjoy it. And don't worry if the cornbread doesn't come out of the slow cooker easily. It tastes just as good in warm crumbly chunks as it does when cut in perfect squares.

Yield: 6–8 servings   Cook Time: 1½ hours

Two 8-ounce boxes Jiffy cornbread mix

2 eggs

⅔ cup milk

½ cup sour cream

One 10-ounce package frozen corn

1 tablespoon sugar

1 jalapeno pepper, chopped (optional)

Spray a lined slow cooker with nonstick cooking spray. Mix all the ingredients, including the jalapeno if desired, until they are blended. Add the mixture to the slow cooker and cook on high for 1 to 1½ hours. To remove the cornbread, place a plate on top of the slow cooker and turn it upside down until the cake comes loose.

Braised Collard Greens

There's no vegetable more southern than good old collard greens! (Okay, except maybe okra. Or boiled peanuts.) These collards come out of the cooker perfectly tender and full of flavor—with just a kick of spice. Serve with your favorite BBQ.

Yield: 4–6 servings   Cook Time: 6 hours

1½ pounds fresh collard greens

3 pounds ham bones

4 cups chicken broth

1 onion, sliced

¼ cup brown sugar

1 teaspoon red pepper flakes

¼ teaspoon salt

Wash and chop the collard greens, discarding the stems. Add the remaining ingredients to a lined slow cooker and place the greens on top. Cover and cook on low for 6 hours, or until the greens are tender. Remove the bones from the slow cooker—be sure to pull off any remaining meat and return the meat to the slow cooker. Serve with your favorite barbecue.

Corn Succotash

My mother grew up in Iowa, so she knew a thing or two about corn. Toward the end of summer every year she'd drive out of the city where we lived to the local farmer's market and return with an armload of fresh corn—usually the peaches and cream variety, as that was her favorite. This corn succotash is a great way to enjoy the taste of fresh summer corn all year long. Serve in a bowl and top with a handful of Parmesan cheese.

Yield: 4–6 servings   Cooking time: 6 hours

One 16-ounce package frozen whole kernel corn

One 16-ounce package frozen lima beans

One 28-ounce can stewed tomatoes, with juice

One 10-ounce can condensed chicken broth

2 onions, chopped

1 tablespoon garlic

Salt and pepper to taste

Parmesan cheese (optional)

Add all the ingredients to a lined slow cooker. Cook on low for 6 hours. Serve in a bowl or drain and serve on a plate. Top with Parmesan cheese, if desired.

Slow Cooker
Mac & Cheese

Everyone loves a side of mac & cheese—just as much as we love it served as the main entrée! This is a remarkably easy dish with a short cook time. The result is a firm, cheesy side dish that works well with the more intense flavors of barbecue.

Yield: 4 large servings   Cook Time: 3 hours

One 1-pound box elbow macaroni

One 12-ounce can evaporated milk

1 ½ cups whole milk

½ stick of butter

2 eggs, beaten

1 teaspoon salt

1 teaspoon dry mustard

1 teaspoon paprika

4 cups shredded cheddar cheese

Add all the ingredients to a lined slow cooker, reserving one cup of shredded cheddar cheese. Mix the ingredients together. Add the remaining cup of cheese on top. Cook on low for 3 hours, stir, and serve.

Tip: Pasta can overcook quickly, so keep an eye on this recipe around the 2½ hour mark. The pasta is done when all the milk has been absorbed and the pasta is tender.

Index

BONUS!

PERFECT BBQ DESSERTS FROM

SLOW
COOKER
DUMP
DESSERTS

AVAILABLE EVERYWHERE BOOKS ARE SOLD!

Slow Cooker Sweet Peach Cobbler

Oh, sweet baking angels and everything that's good in the world! Thanks for this peach cobbler recipe and the blessings it has bestowed on us! Namely, a satisfyingly sweet and easy recipe that takes nature's best fruit (or one of its best, anyway), cooked to perfection for us to enjoy.

Yield: 8 servings   Cook time: 3 hours

Nonstick spray

Two 15.5-ounce cans peaches, drained

¼ cup dark brown sugar

1 cup biscuit mix

½ cup granulated sugar

¾ cup milk

Line your slow cooker with a liner to make cleanup easier. Spray the liner (or just the insert, if you're not using one) with nonstick spray. Add the drained peaches to the slow cooker. Whisk the brown sugar, biscuit mix, sugar, and the milk together in a bowl until blended. Pour the batter over the peaches. Cover and cook on low for 3 hours. Let stand until set, if needed.

Tip: For a sweet twist, try adding a pinch of cinnamon to the mixture before baking.

Chocolate Chip Brownie Cookie Cake

A combination of brownies and cookies . . . sounds good, right? All you need now is ice cream!

Yield: 8 servings   Cook time: 2½ hours

Nonstick spray

One 18.3-ounce box fudge brownie mix

One 17.5-ounce package chocolate chip cookie mix

1¼ cups milk

8 tablespoons (1 stick) unsalted butter, melted

4 large eggs

1 tablespoon vegetable oil

Vanilla ice cream, for serving

Line your slow cooker with a liner to make cleanup easier. Spray the liner (or just the insert, if you're not using one) with nonstick spray. Mix the remaining ingredients together in a bowl and blend well. Add to the slow cooker. Cook on low for 2½ hours. Serve with vanilla ice cream.

Fourth of July Celebration Cake

This red, white, and blue dessert makes a festive, tasty addition to any backyard barbecue or Fourth of July celebration. Garnish with fresh strawberries and blueberries.

Yield: Makes 6 servings   Cook time: 2½ to 3½ hours

Nonstick spray

One 15.25-ounce box white cake mix

1¼ cups water

½ cup vegetable oil

3 large eggs

1 teaspoon vanilla extract

8 tablespoons (1 stick) unsalted butter, melted

1 cup sliced fresh strawberries

1 cup fresh blueberries

Whipped cream, for serving

Strawberries and blueberries, for garnish

Line your slow cooker with a liner to make cleanup easier. Spray the liner (or just the insert, if you're not using one) with nonstick spray. Mix the cake mix, water, oil, eggs, and vanilla together in a bowl until well blended. Add the melted butter to the slow cooker and pour the batter on top. Add the strawberries and blueberries over the cake batter. Cook on low for 2½ to 3½ hours. Allow to cool and cover with whipped cream. Garnish with additional strawberries and blueberries.

Photo Credits